IMAGES
of America

AFRICAN AMERICANS IN TANGIPAHOA AND ST. HELENA PARISHES

THE CITY OF AMITE, LOUISIANA, 1940S–1950S. Amite was incorporated as a town in 1861 just months after the secession of Louisiana from the Union. Amite serves as the seat of Tangipahoa Parish. On the weekend, African American people would get dressed up to go into town for ice cream cones and shopping. Going to town was a huge event for everyone. (Amite Genealogy Library.)

ON THE COVER: LADIES' MYSTIC CLUB. On July 12, 1956, a group of women met and formed the Ladies' Mystic Club with the idea of encouraging "finer womanhood" and education through community support. It later adopted the name it now bears, the Altruist Civic Organization. The charter members were Christine Greenup, president; Ella Mae Badon, vice president; Esterlee W. Spain, recording secretary; Lizzie Mae Seals, financial secretary; and Venola Simmons, treasurer. (Ella Mae Ashe Badon.)

IMAGES
of America

AFRICAN AMERICANS IN TANGIPAHOA AND ST. HELENA PARISHES

Dr. Antoinette Harrell
Foreword by Leonard Smith III

ARCADIA
PUBLISHING

Published by Arcadia Publishing
Charleston, South Carolina

Printed in the United States of America

Library of Congress Control Number: 2018947820

For all general information, please contact Arcadia Publishing:
Telephone 843-853-2070
Fax 843-853-0044
E-mail sales@arcadiapublishing.com
For customer service and orders:
Toll-Free 1-888-313-2665

Visit us on the Internet at www.arcadiapublishing.com

This book is dedicated to everyone who shared oral history and photographs to preserve the rich history of their ancestors, family members, neighbors in the community, and trailblazers who helped shape these two Louisiana Florida Parishes, and to all who opened up their homes and took out their photo albums and boxes of photographs and allowed me to travel back down memory lane with them.

CONTENTS

FOREWORD

The history of so many African American families can be found in shoeboxes in closets, attics, under beds, or just thrown in dresser drawers. These are pictures of mothers, fathers, grandparents, great-grandparents, cousins, aunts, uncles, friends, and neighbors. They share the views of the good and not so good times, smiles, frowns, and tears. We see people in churches, schools, and the military; on family outings; and earning a living. There are so many stories to be told from these photographs. When viewing these pictures, who knew, for instance, that your daughter resembled your great-aunt Tessie to a tee? Every photograph tells a story of a moment in time. These precious images were captured by both professional and amateur photographers. The photographers might have known who the people in the pictures are. They might have shared great times or sorrowful memories with them. They may have been members of an organization, church, school, or work. Those old mementos from a forgotten time may never be brought out of the dark.

As the photographs gather more dust and are pushed farther back in the closet, and as people die off, memories fade. It becomes more of a challenge to add names to the faces. Many end up in garage sales or flea markets around the country. Some are purchased by collectors, and others buy them just because. The new owners try to put together the pieces of the who, what, when, and where of the photographs. Few are successful. The names are forgotten. As time goes on, these old photographs lose their value with the new owners. In time, no one living can identify anyone in the pictures. These photographs' and mementos' next home is the trash.

This is why books like Images of America: *African Americans in Tangipahoa and St. Helena Parishes* are so important. Photographs are collected from different families in our communities and compiled into one setting. Each family photograph has a unique and varied story to tell. This is a testament that, in spite of our differences, we also share so much in common.

—Leonard Smith III
Historian

ACKNOWLEDGMENTS

I want to start by thanking the almighty creator for guiding me and opening doors for me as I published this book. Secondly, I thank my husband, Wallace, for his constant support and words of encouragement and for cooking all those delicious meals.

Special thanks to Dr. Kingsley B. Garrison, Monteral Harrell-Climmons, Earl and Vera Wheeler, Edwin Temple, Ella Mae Badon, Annie Lee Hurst, and Grace Belvin Walker Perry for sharing so many great photographs for this book. I can't thank Glyniss Vernon Gordon enough for contacting people in Amite and traveling to their homes for images. Thank you to Robert Daniels for sharing oral history of the people of Amite. And last but certainly not least, thanks to Howard Nichols for inspiring and encouraging me to publish this book to preserve the undocumented history and images of the African American people of the Louisiana Florida Parishes.

Dr. Kingsley B. Garrison, Ella Mae Badon, and I discussed the importance of documenting the history of African American people in the Florida Parishes. They both have been my inspiration and motivation for preserving the rich history of so many African American people here.

Special thanks to my four grandchildren, Jo'elle, Connor, Carter, and Chase, for assisting me. They traveled with me to the library, carrying my computer and scanner. They helped me pack my equipment and made sure that I didn't forget anything. One day, when each of you read this book, you will appreciate the legacy you helped to preserve. Carter, your kind words and telling me I could do it meant the world to me.

Thank you to Monteral Harrell-Climmons for editing and proofreading. Without a second thought, she didn't hesitate to assist me in this labor of love.

I would like to express my appreciation and gratitude for each person who unequivocally played a vital role by sharing pictures or oral history. This book would not have been possible without each of you. We all took on the challenge.

Through this book, social media, and the *Nurturing Our Roots* genealogy talk show, I hope to educate every person who wants to learn about the resilient people of Tangipahoa and St. Helena Parishes. This was a labor of love, and all the late-night hours were worth every second to preserve the rich, previously undocumented history of the people who stood tall and persevered in the most challenging times. I wish that I could have used every image that I collected, but it was impossible due to the number of pictures and pages that were allowed.

INTRODUCTION

Two decades ago, I started researching my family history in Tangipahoa and St. Helena Parishes. After countless hours in the genealogy departments of both libraries and looking through research materials and books, I was disappointed to find that there was no information about the African American people who helped cultivate the parishes into what they are today. I left very disappointed and decided to do something about it.

I visited the Southeast Center for Louisiana Studies online to look for African American collections, but to no avail. There were none to be found. Some collections only mentioned freed enslaved people.

Many schools started in community churches. The Rosenwald school in Ponchatoula was called the Ponchatoula Colored School. The Hammond area had the Hammond Colored School. In Amite, there was Westside School, and Roseland had Big Zion School. All of these schools were in Tangipahoa Parish. The oldest African American training school in the nation was the Tangipahoa Parish Colored Training School in Kentwood.

Some of the African American communities in Tangipahoa Parish included Butler Town, Reid Quarters, Hyde Quarters, Clemmons Quarters, Gray's Quarters, and Mill Quarters. I have not heard of any communities in St. Helena that were called "quarters."

I have sat in many homes listening to the oral histories of African American people who gave their own account of the struggles for freedom, equality, and social justice and what they had to endure. In many ways, they are still enduring through these struggles in the Florida Parishes.

Many came from the background of farming, working in the timber mills, and picking cotton from "can't see to can't see." The women worked as domestics in homes. To this day, it is very hard for them to talk about it, and doing so brings back memories they tried to forget. They left the cotton fields for the schools and universities to become educators, elected officials, doctors, nurses, and businessmen and -women.

Going to church services was one way they escaped at least one day out of the week. The women dressed up in their Sunday best, adorned with beautiful hats. Their husbands dressed in their finest suits and hats as well. The children, following their parents' example, would shine their shoes and also put on their Sunday best for church.

Inside their homes were shoeboxes, albums of pictures, documents, and other vital records that held the story of our rich history. I was impressed with the images in every home I visited. Every picture tells a story that did not belong tucked away in a shoebox, trunk, or attic. These pictures and documents will find a new home in this book that will help tell the story and preserve our history.

It was the first time in years that some of the people I met with for this book had pulled out their collections and held a conversation about them. I walked down memory lane with each of them. They each pointed out that the youth today have no interest in our history and they have no idea what the previous generations endured for us to be where we are today.

Prominent African Americans owned their own property and land. They had their own schools, churches, cemeteries, and social organizations. After slavery, African Americans in rural areas knew how important it was to purchase and work their own land. Our story from the Reconstruction era to the present is vital to the history of these two Florida Parishes and the state of Louisiana. Our cultural experiences, religious practices, events, and families helped to shape the parishes and the state.

African American families during slavery, the Jim Crow era, and the civil rights movement endured horrible atrocities and brutal treatment daily. Local civil rights leaders championed the causes that many people intentionally disregarded or were too afraid to take a stand on. They stood up in the face of racism and injustice to make these parishes a better place to live for African American people.

African Americans in both parishes fought for equal education in Tangipahoa Parish. My grandfather Jasper Harrell used his pickup truck to take African American people to the voting polls. Collis Temple Sr. refused to allow his children to attend the fair in Amite on Saturdays because it was called "Nigger Day." Instead, he started a fair for African American people in Kentwood.

My second great-grandfather Robert and his son Alexander purchased 200 acres in 1888 for their family. Buying land was just as important as getting an education. Many could not read or write but made their mark (X) on legal documents. A man named Robert "Free Bob" Vernon who could not read or write purchased over 2,300 acres in Arcola, Louisiana. He donated land for the school, church, and cemetery.

We stand on the shoulders of our ancestors, many of whom we will never know about or ever hear their stories. This is how we can continue to thrive today, becoming engineers, doctors, entrepreneurs, men and women of the gospels, authors, businessmen and -women, television hosts, educators, elected officials, servicemen and -women, law enforcers, and productive citizens of the parishes.

This book is designed to illustrate the political, social, religious, educational, and cultural events of African Americans of Tangipahoa and St. Helena Parishes. It is impossible to use all the images I have collected over two decades. The images were chosen according to the outline of each chapter. Publishing this book is a sure way to be certain that African American history in these parishes will not be erased nor destroyed. Our story, our history, and our experiences must be told by us.

One

African American Families in Louisiana's Florida Parishes

In 1832, the southern section of St. Helena Parish was taken from Livingston Parish, and the courthouse was moved from Montpelier to Greensburg, where it remains today. Tangipahoa Parish was organized in 1869, during Reconstruction. Land was taken from Livingston, St. Helena, St. Tammany, and Washington Parishes. The name "Tangipahoa" comes from an Acolapissa word meaning "ear of corn" or "those who gather corn." The African American population comprised about a quarter of the population overall in the Florida Parishes before the war. The city of Amite is the Tangipahoa Parish seat.

Many African American families live in these two Louisiana Florida Parishes. After slavery was abolished in 1863, many families remained tied to the parishes. St. Helena was the largest slaveholding parish of the Florida Parishes. The following African American surnames are still present today: Addison, Amacker, Ashe, Atkins, Badon, Banks, Bates, Batiste, Bennett, Boykins, Bridge, Brooks, Brown, Brumfield, Bryant, Buckhalter, Burton, Butler, Calihan, Carter, Chaney, Chapman, Clark, Coleman, Collins, Coney, Cook, Cotton, Crier, Crook, Curtis, Cyprian, Daniels, Dillon, Doughty, Dudley, Dunn, Dykes, Edwards, Elliot, Finn, Fluker, Foster, Francois, Frazier, Freeman, Galmon, Garrison, Gordon, Gorman, Hall, Harrell, Harris, Harrison, Hart, Higginbottom, Hill, Hitchen, Holden, Holiday, Holmes, Hookfin, Huff, Hurst, Hutchinson, Irving, Jackson, James, Johnson, Kemp, Kendrick, Landrew, Lawson, Lee, Leonard, Lewis, Lloyd, Lucky, Mabry, Magee, Martin, Mason, McCay, McClendon, McCoy, McKnight, Milton, Montgomery, Moore, Morris, Muse, Nettles, Parker, Perry, Pitts, Ponds, Pool, Pope, Porter, Pounds, Quinn, Ricard, Richardson, Robertson, Robinson, Rudison, Sanders, Selder, Self, Sims, Smith, Solomon, Sopher, Spears, Steptoe, Stevens, Stevenston, Stewart, Stickland, Stokes, Sutton, Tanner, Tate, Temple, Thomas, Thompson, Tillery, Tolliver, Topps, Tucker, Vernon, Vining, Wall, Walker, Warner, Warren, Washington, Wells, West, Wheat, Wheeler, Williams, Wilson, Womack, Wren, Wright, and Zanders.

Little 25 Club, 1950s–1960s. The Little 25 Club comprised women who lived in Tangipahoa Parish. The club organized many social and civic events. Ella Mae Badon is seated at left, Laura Knighten is seated at right, and Ruby Ashe Lowe is standing at left. (Ella Mae Ashe Badon.)

Emma Mead Harrell and Her Children, 1940s. Born in 1864, Emma purchased land for her family in 1896, long before women's suffrage in 1920. Emma was a farmer in Amite. From left to right are (seated) Alex Harrell, Emma, Bertha, and Ella; (standing) Edgar, Jasper, Palmer, Henry, and Theodore. The boy on the porch is unidentified. (Monteral Harrell-Climmons.)

LENA SELF TEMPLE, 1970s. Lena was married to Charlie Temple. After her husband died, she stayed on the 54-acre homestead and continued farming. She sold her produce to Ardillo Supermarket in Amite. (Edwin Temple.)

CORA WHEELER TEMPLE, 1950s. Cora was one of John and Letha Washington Wheeler's daughters. She was married to Stanley Temple. They raised their family in New Orleans. Cora worked in the school cafeteria until she retired. Pictured are Cora and her triplets (in unknown order), Bernard, Bertrand, and Burrell Temple. (Earl Wheeler.)

HARRELL SIBLINGS, 1970s. The Harrell siblings are the children of Jasper Harrell Sr. and Josephine Richardson Harrell. The family was celebrating youngest daughter Delores Harrell's college graduation. She was the first in her family to graduate from college. From left to right are Jasper Jr., Delores, Frank, Isabel, Henry, and Roosevelt Harrell. (Monteral Harrell-Climmons.)

FAMILY OF COLTIS TEMPLE SR., 1970s. Collis Temple Sr. was married to Shirley Cross. He was the second principal at O.W. Dillon School in Kentwood. Their son Collis Temple Jr. was the first African American basketball player at Louisiana State University. Pictured are Shirley Cross Temple and Collis Temple Sr. with their daughters and son Collis Temple Jr. (Edwin Temple.)

EXTENDED HARRELL FAMILY, 1960s. Some of the Harrell family took part in the Great Migration to the North in search of a better life. Six million African Americans left the South. Harrell family members are pictured here. Farm life was not for Bertha (far right). (Monteral Harrell-Climmons.)

THE RICHARDSON FAMILY, 1970s. The Richardson family are the descendants of Alexander and Melissa Wheat Richardson, who had one daughter and nine sons. Alexander Richardson obtained only a third-grade education and worked his way to owning Richardson Funeral Home. From left to right are (first row) Pete, Emmitt, Helenstine, Earl Lee, and Joseph; (second row) unidentified, Walter, Nathaniel, Samuel, and Darnell Richardson. (Alex Richardson.)

ALEXANDER RICHARDSON SR. AND WIFE MELISSA WHEAT RICHARDSON. Born in 1907, Alexander worked on WPA projects during the Depression, including cutting the right-of-way for the Montpelier to Greensburg Highway. With his supporting wife at his side, he decided in the late 1950s or early 1960s to open his own funeral home and insurance agency in Amite. (Richardson Funeral Home.)

CARRIE MCKNIGHT AND FAMILY, 1950s. Carrie worked hard as a domestic worker for prominent white families in Amite. She was determined for her children to become successful. She is pictured with her daughter Alma Harrison Vernon and her sons (from left to right) Robert, Nathaniel, and Johnny. Daughter Bell Azora is not pictured. "I remember my grandmother being very stern," said Glyniss Gordon. (Glyniss Vernon Gordon.)

THE DUNN FAMILY, 1960s. The Dunn children are descendants of Theodore and Gladys Chapman Dunn. Theodore and Gladys left Amite County, Mississippi, on a mule and wagon and moved to Kentwood, where Theodore purchased land and started farming. (Paulette Gilmore Sims.)

THEODORE DUNN SR. AND GLADYS CHAPMAN DUNN, 1950s. Theodore was born in Amite County, Mississippi. He was a farmer and logger who purchased land in Kentwood to farm and build a home for his wife and children. He was killed in a truck accident in Liverpool, Louisiana, in the late 1950s. (Paulette Gilmore Sims.)

Jasper Harrell Jr. and Primrose Bennett Wedding, 1958. Jasper and Primrose are pictured on their special day. In the front row are Jasper's nieces and nephews (from left to right) James, Diane, and Jo-Ann Lewis. The bridesmaid on the left is Primrose's sister Mariah Bennett. Standing next to the bride is Jasper's sister Isabel Harrell. The bridesmaid on the right is Jasper's cousin Betty Jackson. In the back are Jasper's brother Roosevelt Harrell Sr. (left) and Jasper's cousin Eddie Jackson Jr. (second from left). (Monteral Harrell-Climmons.)

Juanita Harrell and Friends, 1950s. Born in 1922 in New Orleans to Edgar and Minnie Nolan Harrell, Juanita was a seamstress and secretary and a lifelong member of Petty AME Church in New Orleans. (Antoinette Harrell.)

TONEY BUSH AND WIFE MAMIE BUSH, 1950s–1960s. Pictured here attending their daughter Juanita's wedding, Toney and Mamie lived their entire lives in Amite. (The Bush family.)

THE CUTRER FAMILY, 1980s. The Cutrer family is descended from Robert "Free Bob" Vernon; his daughter married into the Cutrer family. The Cutrers were educators. "Free Bob" Vernon donated land for the Mount Canaan Church and School in Arcola, Louisiana. (Fairy Dean Cutrer Hannibal.)

EUGENE PONDS AND HIS YOUNG WIFE, IDA DAVIS, 1940S. Eugene Ponds was born in 1887 in Plaquemine, Louisiana. He left the plantation during Reconstruction to follow sawmill work. He moved to Ponchatoula to work at Louisiana Lumber Company. Ida Davis, many years his junior, was born in 1915 in Mississippi. After she married Eugene Ponds and moved to Ponchatoula, she picked and packed strawberries and did domestic work. Later she became a self-taught hairdresser. (Eddie Ponds.)

THE FOSTER COUPLE, 1970S. Mattie Edward Foster was William Sherman Foster's second wife. They were sharecroppers. William had large families with both of his wives. (Raymond Foster Sr.)

Monroe Perry and Allie Brown, 1940s–1950s. Born in 1895 in St. Helena Parish, Monroe Perry worked a 40-acre farm with mules and his tools. He planted and harvested vegetables for shipping and sale at the local markets. During the off seasons, he made sugarcane syrup at Battles' Syrup Mill on Bennett Road for local farmers. (Helen Perry Edwards.)

Jake and Martha Boykins, 1920s–1930s. Jake Boykins was born in 1867 in the Fifth Ward in St. Helena Parish to Sam and Catherine Boykins. He and Martha were farmers in Fluker, Louisiana. He did not attend school but knew how to read and write. According to Roy Curtis, Jake was a strong voice for justice in the community. (Linnie Walls.)

WALTER AND ADA COLEMAN WREN. Walter Wren made a living for himself and family by farming. It was more of a hobby than a living, because he enjoyed it so much. He planted strawberries, watermelons, greens, snap beans, squash, sweet potatoes, peanuts, cucumbers, peppers, okra, and cotton, and also owned a cotton gin. Ada worked as a nurse at Lallie Kemp Charity Hospital in Independence, Louisiana. (Walter Wren III.)

DR. PERCY L. WALKER AND WIFE GRACE WALKER, 1970S. Born in 1918, Percy Walker graduated from Southern University in agriculture education and Tuskegee University in veterinary medicine. He graduated from officer training school and served in World War II and the Korean War as a first lieutenant. After his service years, he was a substitute teacher, social worker, and government meat inspector. He established an Amite veterinary clinic in 1953 and continued his practice until 1995. (Grace Sanders Walker Perry.)

GLENIS THOMPSON LANDREW AND JAMES ALEXIS WEDDING, 1960s–1970s. Glenis was a domestic worker and lifelong resident of Amite, where she raised her children. (Monteral Harrell-Climmons.)

JERRY DEAN LANDREW AND PATRICIA LANDREW, 1960s. Jerry Dean (left) and Patricia are sisters. Jerry Dean was a baker. She married twice, first to Raymond Harrell Sr., and had two children with him, Monteral Harrell and Raymond Jr. (Monteral Harrell-Climmons.)

BISHOP WILLIE K. GORDON SR. AND ALMA RICHARDSON GORDON, 1960s. Born in 1909 in St. Helena Parish, Willie Gordon donated a half acre to build a church, Gordon Chapel Church of God in Christ. The church became a school as well. The first teacher was Luberta Butler Temple. Alma was a homemaker. The Gordons were the parents of seven children. (Cletis Gordon Sr.)

ALLEN AND PHEBY SELF VINING, 1920s. Allen Vining was born in St. Helena to Frank and Martha Green Vining. Frank was held as a slave on a plantation in St. Helena. Allen was a farmer by occupation. He was married twice, first to Rosa Hart and then to Pheby Self Vining. Allen passed away in 1928. (Edwin Temple.)

FESTUSS MIX WALKER AND COREAN BRIGSS WALKER, 1920–1930s. The Walkers were parents of the first African American veterinarian on the north end of Tangipahoa Parish, Dr. Percy Walker. (Grace Belvins Walker Perry.)

JOSEPH AND GENORA JOHNSON WHEELER, 1980s. The Wheelers married in the 1940s. Genora was born in St. Helena. She and her family were sharecroppers. After she married Joseph, they lived in Amite. Joseph was a farmer and bus driver. He also owned his own truck company and the Dew Drop Inn in Amite. Genora went to all the funerals in St. Helena and Tangipahoa. She had a very rich collection of photographs and funeral programs. (Earl Wheeler.)

EDDIE JACKSON AND ELLA CASON JACKSON, 1960s–1970s. Eddie Jackson Jr. was the family photographer for the Richardson, Harrell, Vining, Williams, Jackson, and Temple families. After his death, none of his images was located. His wife, Ella Cason, taught school in the Tangipahoa Parish school system. (Monteral Harrell-Climmons.)

REV. LEE WOOLRIDGE AND SELINA WOOLRIDGE, 1950s. Born in 1889 in St. Helena, Lee Woolridge was self-employed as a farmer in Montpelier, Louisiana. He was an amputee, and made his own prosthesis. He was married to Selina Woolridge and was the father of Laura Knighten, Irene Lee, Clara Woolridge, Mary Brown, Rosa Lee Brown, and Delia Mae Woolridge Garrison. (Dr. Kingsley B. Garrison.)

ISABEL HARRELL COOK AND CHILDREN, 2013. Born in 1939 to Jasper and Josephine Richardson Harrell, Isabel is known for her strawberry cake and homemade yeast rolls. From left to right are Thomas Cook, Michael Cook, Antoinette Harrell, Isabel Harrell Cook, and Reginald Cook. Antoinette is the host of *Nurturing Our Roots*, a television talk show. (Antoinette Harrell.)

CLEVELAND AND LILLIE LOU HITCHEN BENNETT, 1970s. Cleveland Bennett served in World War II. After being discharged, he moved back to St. Helena and started farming. Though he only had a fourth-grade education, he was very wise and was a great provider for his wife and family. Lillie worked right alongside her husband, canned all the produce, and stocked her shelves. Her favorite place was sitting in her chair in front of the wood-burning fireplace. (Wanda Harrell Knighten.)

THE PUGH FAMILY, 1970s. The Pugh family came from Arkansas to start a church in the 1940s or 1950s. Rev. Ernest Thomas Pugh was the pastor of Butler Zion AME Church in Amite. He taught music to the children in the community. Several of his children followed in his shoes as musicians and educators. His daughter Carrie taught music in the Tangipahoa Parish school system until she retired. (Carrie Pugh-Paul.)

HILDA "ZEMORA" VINING AND FAMILY. Born in 1922 to the late Caleb Ike Vining and Eva Ellen Vining, she was one of five sisters: Christine Williams, Florence Warner, Creola Anderson, Francis Woolridge, and Hilda R. Pikes. A lifelong resident of Montpelier, she attended Bear Creek School and married at the early age of 13. (Annie Lee Hurst.)

Two

EDUCATION IN TANGIPAHOA AND ST. HELENA PARISHES

During slavery, many African Americans were denied access to education. Anyone caught with a book in their hands could be beaten, murdered, or sold off the plantation. After slavery was abolished, the newly freed former slaves wanted their children to learn how to read and write. They wanted to send their children to school, although in some rural communities schools were located far away from their homes. They would often walk miles with no shoes and little to eat to attend school in a church or a one-room building. One of the earliest works that specifically dealt with black education in general was W.E.B. Dubois's *Black Reconstruction in America: 1860–1880.* James D. Anderson provides a comprehensive study of the development of schools for African Americans in *The Education of Blacks in the South.*

Some of the schools available to African Americans were Ponchatoula Colored School, Westside Elementary and High School, Perrin High School, Hammond Colored School, Big Zion School, Woodland School, Amite Colored School, Tangipahoa Parish Colored Training School, Greenville High School, Rocky Hill Church School, Gordon Chapel Church of God in Christ, and the Colored Citizens School.

"The older people wanted you to learn how to read and write," said Dr. Kingsley B. Garrison. That was very important to them, he said. Many schools were established by men such as Armstead Strange, Prof. O.W. Dillon, and Prof. David Charles Reeves. Sometimes, the men would go from door to door in the African American community, talking to parents and encouraging them to allow their children to get an education. Julius Rosenwald became interested in the welfare of blacks and established the Julius Rosenwald Fund, which had to be spent within 25 years of his death to better conditions through education. More than 5,000 Rosenwald schools were established for African Americans in 15 Southern states, including Louisiana.

PONCHATOULA COLORED SCHOOL, 1930s. This school was located in Ponchatoula, Louisiana. Photographs like this one are very rare. (Ella Mae Ashe Badon.)

PONCHATOULA COLORED SCHOOL, 1947. Pictured is the Ponchatoula graduating class of 1947 with Prof. David Charles Reeves. (Dr. Kingsley B. Garrison.)

PONCHATOULA COLORED SCHOOL, 1956. Pictured is the Ponchatoula graduating class of 1956. (Dr. Kingsley B. Garrison)

PERRIN HIGH SCHOOL EDUCATORS, 1960s. Perrin High School is in Ponchatoula. From left to right are (first row) Joan Seals, Estelle Cable, Viola Carter, Florida Smith, Elizabeth McCray, Ethleen Fleet, Ruby Ashe Lowe, and Lovie D. Garrison; (second row) Wilona Terrence, Edna Bean, Laura Knighten, Lillen James, Ella Mae Badon, Otis Watson, Genois Reeve, Anna Starwood, Curtis Warner, Mary Lee Carter, Riley Wilson, and Gideon Carter. (Ella Mae Ashe Badon.)

AMITE COLORED SCHOOL, 1940s. The little wood-framed school was located in Butler Town. These were the children of farmers and sharecroppers. From left to right in the first row are unidentified, Delores Zanders, Rosa Lawson, unidentified, Rachel McCoy, Audra Harrell, and two unidentified. Also pictured are Catherine Harrell (third row, third from left), and principal Willie Martin (third row, far right). (Rev. Raymond Foster Sr.)

AMITE GIRLS' BASKETBALL TEAM, 1950s. The Amite team was one of the best in the district. This photograph sits on the dresser in Yvonne Collins's bedroom. Yvonne, standing second from left, was very proud of her team. Standing at far right is Augustine Perry, and the girl kneeling second from right is Amanda Bush. (Yvonne Collins.)

WESTSIDE HIGH SCHOOL BOYS' BASKETBALL TEAM, 1960s. Westside High's team was very competitive and played hard. Westside High School was segregated until 1969. Coach Willard Vernon is kneeling in the first row. (Glyniss Vernon Gordon.)

WESTSIDE HIGH SCHOOL BAND, 1960s. Westside High School was known to have one of the best bands and prettiest majorettes under the direction of Edwin Duplesis, head band director at Westside High in Amite from 1955 to 1970. He led the marching and symphonic bands to state competitions and brought a lot of attention to Amite. (Gracie Belvins Walker Perry.)

WESTSIDE ELEMENTARY QUEEN AND HER COURT, LATE 1950s. Glyniss Vernon was crowned queen at Amite Elementary School. She grew up to become an educator like her parents, Alma Harrison and Dr. Willard Vernon. Many members of her extended family were also educators. (Glyniss Vernon Gordon.)

WESTSIDE HIGH SCHOOL QUEEN AND HER ESCORT, 1959. Carrie Pugh was crowned queen in 1959. She played music and chose music teaching as a career, following in the footsteps of her father, Ernest Thomas Pugh. (Carrie Pugh-Paul.)

TANGIPAHOA PARISH TRAINING SCHOOL, 1940s. Founded in 1911 by Armstead Strange, this was the first training school for blacks in the entire South and one of the first rural public schools providing secondary education for blacks in the nation. The school was expanded in 1918 by Prof. Oliver Wendell Dillon. Pictured are Clothilde Dancer and her class. (Gracie Belvins Walker Perry.)

TANGIPAHOA PARISH TRAINING SCHOOL, 1940s. Students are pictured with their teacher, Ernestine L. Imes. (Grace Belvins Walker Perry.)

STATE OF LOUISIANA

Class--AA

Department of Education

State Approved Negro High School

DIPLOMA

THIS CERTIFIES THAT

Arizola Earnest

has satisfactorily completed the Course of Study required by the State. This Diploma is awarded as evidence of scholastic attainments and good character and as a testimonial of graduation from Tangipahoa Parish Training *School at* Kentwood *Louisiana.*

Given this 4th day of April 1946

Approved:

J. E. Williams
State Supervisor of Negro Education

R. R. Emery
State Director of Elementary
and Secondary Education

Jno. E. Coxe
State Superintendent of Public Education

S. A. Mitchell
President Parish School Board

Superintendent Parish Schools

Principal

TANGIPAHOA PARISH TRAINING SCHOOL DIPLOMA, 1946. The Louisiana Department of Education issued this diploma to Arizola Earnest. (Arizola Earnest.)

TANGIPAHOA PARISH TRAINING SCHOOL QUEEN, 1950s–1960s. Fairy Dean Cutrer was the crowned queen. She chose education as a career. (Fairy Dean Cutrer Hannibal.)

St. Helena High School, 1962. Annie Lee Vining Hurst (far right) was chosen for the St. Helena High School homecoming court. The girls in the court are, from left to right, Sally Ann Gorman, Jeanelle Atkins Rankins, Linda Freeman, and Florene Butler. (Annie Lee Vining Hurst)

Southern University Homecoming Court, 1965. Annie was chosen Miss Magnolia Triangles. Her escort was Melvin Edward, who was also from St. Helena Parish. (Annie Lee Vining Hurst.)

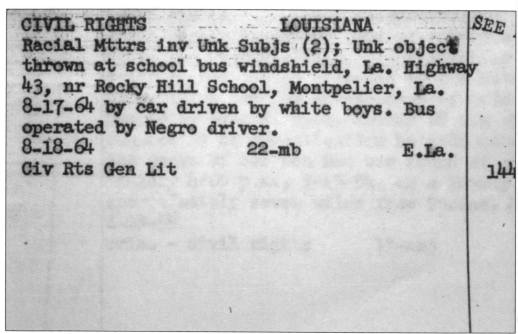

RACIAL INCIDENT NEAR ROCKY HILL SCHOOL, 1964. On August 17, 1964, two unknown objects were thrown from a car driven by a white boy at the windshield of a school bus driven by an African American on State Highway 43 near Rocky Hill School in Montpelier. (National Archives.)

MOUNT CANAAN SCHOOL IN ARCOLA. Robert "Free Bob" Vernon donated the land for the first school for African American children in Arcola. The school officially closed its doors in the mid-1960s, according to the oral history of Tony Stone. (Luther Tolliver.)

ORA LEE FINN, EDUCATOR IN THE TANGIPAHOA PARISH SCHOOL SYSTEM, 1970s–1980s. Ora was a mentor for many students in Tangipahoa Parish schools. She was the principal of Amite High School. (Schirra Finn.)

GINGER VERNON FRANCOIS, EDUCATOR IN THE TANGIPAHOA PARISH SCHOOL SYSTEM. Ginger was a principal at Kentwood High School and Amite High School in Tangipahoa Parish. (Schirra Finn.)

WESTSIDE HIGH SCHOOL BARBER GRADUATING CLASS, 1955. The young men in this photograph are posing for their class picture. According to L.J. Brumfield, this was a military class graduating at Westside High School. He had already served in the Korean War and returned home. He received a small check to go back to school. Edwin Wilson was the instructor for Tangipahoa Parish Training School in Kentwood, and Willie Martin was the instructor for Westside High. (Myrtle Cook.)

GORDON CHAPEL CHURCH OF GOD IN CHRIST SCHOOL, FIRST EDUCATOR, 1930s–1940s. Ida Luberta was born about 1884 in Louisiana. She completed the fourth year of high school and was hired to teach school at Gordon Chapel Church of God in Christ. She was the wife of John Temple, who was born about 1873 and was a farmer by occupation. (James Daniels.)

ROBERT POPE, 1970s. Robert Pope, born in St. Helena Parish, was an educator in the parish's schools. (Shan Gordon.)

MAMIE BUSH EVANS, 1935. Mamie was born in Tangipahoa Parish and taught in the parish's school system. She graduated from Southern University in Baton Rouge with a bachelor of arts degree. (Rev. Raymond Foster Sr.)

SPEECH SPECIALIST, 2018. Monteral Harrell-Climmons is the daughter of the late Elder Raymond Harrell Sr. and Jerry Dean Landrew Harrell. She married Walter Climmons and has two children, Darius Harrell and Tyra Climmons. She attended Grambling State University and obtained a bachelor of science degree in speech and language pathology in 1996. She has been employed in the field of speech pathology for 21 years. She is an active member of the Tau Iota Omega Chapter of Alpha Kappa Alpha Sorority in Slidell, Louisiana, where she currently serves as scholarship chair. (Antoinette Harrell.)

PRIMROSE BENNETT HARRELL, 1970s. Primrose attended elementary school in a wooden church school in St. Helena Parish and graduated from St. Helena Parish Colored Training School (high school) in 1953. She furthered her formal education at Southern University in Baton Rouge. There, she obtained a bachelor of science degree in vocational home economics in 1957. She later earned a bachelor of arts degree in secondary education and pursued additional studies at Dillard and Southeastern Louisiana Universities. (Wanda Harrell Knighten.)

FRED AND VERNIA McCOY, 1980s. Fred and his wife, Vernia, were both educators. Fred fought for justice as an educator in the Tangipahoa school system. He filed a lawsuit and won the case during integration. Later, he became principal at Midway School in Natalbany. Vernia served 32 years as a classroom teacher. She also coached the girls' basketball team at Westside Middle School. (Vernia McCoy.)

FORCHIA VARNADO WILSON, 1950s. Forchia was a graduate of the Tangipahoa Parish Training School who came to Kentwood from Rose Hill, Mississippi, to serve as a home economics teacher. She graduated from the Tuskegee Institute in Alabama and later studied at Columbia University. She received her master's degree in education from Southern University in Baton Rouge. As a high school teacher, she taught culinary arts and sewing classes. She sponsored clubs and student trips for many years. (Marcia Wilson.)

PRISCILLA POPE GORDON, 1950s–1960s.
Priscilla was educated and taught in the
St. Helena Parish school system. She
married Willie K. Gordon Sr., and they
had one daughter. (Shan Gordon.)

**DR. KINGSLEY BLAINE AND DELIA MAE
W. GARRISON, 1950s–1960s.** They both
taught in Tangipahoa Parish schools until
they retired. Dr. Garrison is donating
his rich photograph collection to the
Southeastern Center for Louisiana
Studies. (Dr. Kingsley B. Garrison.)

HELEN PERRY EDWARDS, 1960S–1970S. Helen taught second grade at Westside Elementary until integration. She is a lifelong resident of Amite and is the mother of one son, Eric Edwards. (Helen Perry Edwards.)

ALMA HARRISON VERNON, 1960s. Alma spent her life educating, empowering, and inspiring women throughout Tangipahoa and St. Helena Parishes. She received her elementary and high school education in Tangipahoa Parish before getting a bachelor of science degree in elementary education from Grambling State University. She taught in the Tangipahoa Parish school system. (Glyniss Vernon Gordon.)

Joshua Williams Sr., 1960s–1970s.
Joshua Williams Sr. was the principal of Burgher School and the first African American councilman elected to serve on the Amite City Council, in the late 1970s. (Grace Belvins Walker Perry.)

Reginald Cotton Sr., 1980s. Born in 1923, Cotton served as head football coach of Kentwood High School from 1949 to 1954. He coached at Westside High School from 1954 to 1960 and at Amite High School from 1969 to 1980. He also served as assistant principal at Amite High School. Cotton served three years as a corporal in the US Marines and was honorably discharged in 1946. In 1980, he was elected to the parish school board as a member from District B. (Grace Belvins Walker Perry.)

LEVORIA POPE STEWART, 1960s. Levoria was educated in the St. Helena Parish school system and later taught in the system. Her husband, John, was an agriculturist. John raised livestock and bred certain types of meat. He was also a machinist and repaired the local farmers' equipment. (Shan Gordon.)

MILDRED RICARD, 2000s. Mildred Ricard taught first grade for 36 years at Westside Elementary and Amite Elementary until she retired. (Mildred Ricard.)

MAGGIE ALDRIDGE, 1950s. Maggie was the first African American supervisor in the Tangipahoa Parish school system. She was also the president of the Gladiolus Club and the pianist for Mount Canaan Baptist Church, Little Bethel Baptist Church, and Grant Chapel AME Church. She was very instrumental in getting the *Louisiana Weekly* paper sold and distributed in the African American communities. (Fairy Dean Cutrer Hannibal.)

DR. SAMUEL RICHARDSON AND DOROTHY J. RICHARDSON, 1990. Dr. Richardson and his wife were both educators in the Tangipahoa Parish school system. He was a principal of Hammond Junior High and a school board member of the Tangipahoa Parish school system. He was also the founder of Gordon-Richardson Christian Academy in Amite. (Antoinette Harrell.)

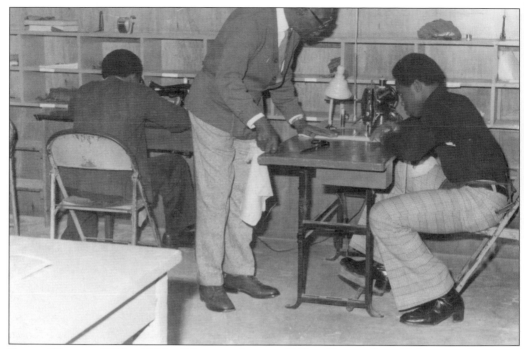

EDWIN WILSON, 1950s–1960s. Edwin was born in 1918 in Phenix City, Alabama, and received two bachelor of science degrees in 1949 from Tuskegee Institute. He was an active member of Alpha Phi Alpha fraternity and received a master's degree from Southern University. He served as an assistant principal and tailoring instructor at Kentwood High School. (Marcia Wilson.)

CARRIE PUGH-PAUL, 1960s. Carrie taught music in the Tangipahoa Parish school system until she retired. (Carrie Pugh-Paul.)

EDUCATORS' CONVENTION MEETING, 1948. Educators took pride in teaching their students. Often, they would attend educators' workshops and conferences to learn new teaching techniques to bring back to their classes. (Fairy Dean Cutrer Hannibal.)

SOUTHERN UNIVERSITY AGRICULTURE DEPARTMENT, 1950s–1960s. Southern University, the largest historically African American university in Louisiana, was chartered in 1880 in New Orleans as a state-supported institution for the education of African Americans. The 1890 Morrill Act allowed Southern to be designated a land grant institution and established an agricultural and mechanical department. (Glyniss Vernon Gordon.)

Supt. Emmitt N. Richardson Sr. and His Son Emmitt Richardson Jr., 2017. Born in Amite to Gordon Chapel Church of God in Christ superintendent Alexander and Melissa Wheat Richardson, Emmitt N. Richardson Sr. and his wife, Carolyn, organized several missions to Haiti to help those in need. (Antoinette Harrell.)

Three

AFRICAN AMERICAN CHURCHES

African American churches play a vital role in their communities. Every Sunday morning, families gather for their Sunday meeting. Women dress with hats and gloves, men in their Sunday suits, and their children in their best dress, and they head to their places of worship. In 1867, Rev. Arthur Tasker, a former slave, established Tasker AME Church in Ponchatoula. Just a few miles away, another former slave, Charles Daggs, established the Greater St. James AME Church. Daggs was brought to New Orleans on a ship called the *Tribune* in 1835. He stated on his pension application that he was owned by Henry Johnson, a former governor of Louisiana.

Solomon Johnson, a slave, asked his master's permission to build a "brush-harber" on what was then a plantation. The permission was granted in 1863; documented evidence attesting to the brush arbor remains in the records at the courthouse in Amite. Today, the church, in Roseland, is called Big Zion AME Church. Other churches in the African American communities are Ard Chapel AME, Bethel Tabernacle, Black Creek AME, Brown Chapel Church, Butler AME Zion, Emanuel Church of God in Christ (COGIC), Fluker Chapel AME, Gordon Harrell COGIC, Gordon-Richardson Temple of Deliverance COGIC, Grant Chapel AME, Lazard Church, Little Bethel Baptist Church, Macedonia Missionary Baptist Church, Mount Canaan Missionary Baptist Church, Mount Zion Freewill Baptist Church, Oak Grove AME, Orange Grove COGIC, Pope Memorial COGIC, Quinn Chapel, Rocky Hill AME, Rose Valley Church, Sweet Home Baptist Church, St. Joseph Missionary Baptist Church, St. Paul Missionary Baptist Church, and Turner Chapel AME.

MOUNT CANAAN BAPTIST CHOIR, 1950s–1960s. Fairy Dean Cutrer Hannibal recalled the days when her aunt Lettie Anderson would get the choir together to practice and sing. Fairy was a little girl when this photograph was taken. She is standing in the front, behind the girl at the podium. Her aunt Lettie is standing in the back at left. (Fairy Dean Cutrer Hannibal.)

GOOD HOPE MISSIONARY BAPTIST CHURCH BAPTISMAL, 1950s–1960s. It was common for African American churches to baptize worshipers in the rivers. Their heritage consists of river baptism in the earlier 20th century. (Dr. Kingsley B. Garrison.)

GOOD HOPE MISSIONARY BAPTIST CHURCH, 1940s. The children and their Sunday School teacher pose to have their picture taken. The church is located in Ponchatoula. (Dr. Kingsley B. Garrison.)

ST. PAUL BAPTIST CHURCH. This church was established in Hammond. (Earline Dangerfield.)

COMMUNITY CHURCH OF GOD IN CHRIST, 1990s. This church was established in 1994 in Amite. (Rev. Raymond Foster Sr.)

LITTLE BETHEL BAPTIST CHURCH, 1960s–1970s. Little Bethel began with a few dedicated followers in a small log cabin one mile west of its present site. Some of the pioneer members were Sister Rosa Butler, Sister Frances Johnson, and Sister Betsy Carpenter; Rev. Guy Beck and Rev. Newton Johnson were the leaders. In 1881, Rev. Riley Vernon officially organized this group into the Little Bethel Baptist Church. He was the first official pastor, with those named above as charter members. (Glyniss Vernon Gordon.)

GORDON CHAPEL CHURCH OF GOD IN CHRIST, 1980s–1990s. This church was established in the 1930s in Amite. Several of the earliest members were the Pounds, Richardson, Harrell, Brooks, Coleman, Wren, Wheat, Bennett, Landrew, and Gordon families. Pictured are Supt. Samuel Richardson (center) and Elder Raymond Harrell (left). Behind them, the church choir is singing a song of praise. (Monteral Harrell-Climmons.)

SHADY GROVE EASTERN STARS, 1950s–1960s. Shady Grove Chapter 134, Order of the Eastern Star, met in Fluker. Sitting on the right is Vernia McCoy. She served Chapter 134 for 47 years. (Vernia McCoy.)

ORANGE GROVE CHURCH OF GOD IN CHRIST, 1960s–1970s. This church is located in Kentwood. Marie Gordon is second from left in the first row. Pastor Alonzo Richardson and his wife, Missionary Mary Richardson (to his left), are at center in the second row. (Supt. Jimmy Richardson.)

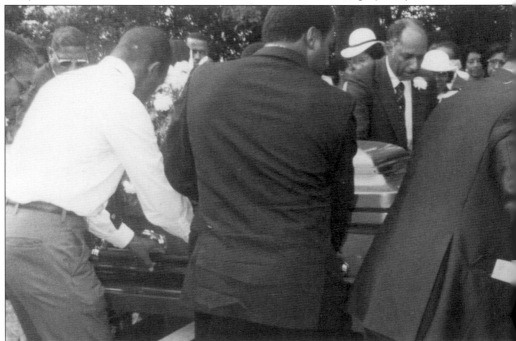

FUNERAL OF ELDER JASPER HARRELL JR., 1987. Elder Jasper Harrell Jr. was born in 1934 in Amite. He was a preacher and truck driver by occupation. He lived his life between Baton Rouge and Amite. (Antoinette Harrell.)

A.C. Evans, Architect, 1950s. An obituary for architect A.C. Evans in the July 31, 1936, issue of the *Vindicator* newspaper read: "Death claims a Good Colored citizen here. Death last Friday morning at one o'clock claimed A.C. Evans, one of the best known colored citizens, who has resided here for thirty years." Evans took much interest in church work. He was born in 1875 and married Mattie Holloway. (Juan Rigo Castille.)

Greater St. James AME Church, 2017. Rev. Charles Daggs established the Greater St. James AME Church in Hammond in 1867. It was the first African American church in the town. Charles Daggs was brought to New Orleans on a slave ship named the *Tribune* on October 1, 1835. (Antoinette Harrell.)

59

GORDON CHAPEL CHURCH OF GOD IN CHRIST, 1980s. In 1930, Bishop Willie K. Gordon donated a half acre to the people to build a church. The church is on the grounds where a brush arbor had been built. The first pastor of the newly established church was Elder James Edwards. From left to right are Supt. Samuel Richardson, Elder Roosevelt Harrell Sr., and Bishop James Earl Gordon. (Antoinette Harrell.)

ORGAN PLAYING AT GORDON CHAPEL CHURCH OF GOD IN CHRIST, 1990s. Nathaniel Richardson Sr. plays the organ at the church where his father, Supt. Alexander Richardson, and his brother, Supt. Samuel Richardson, pastored until they passed away. (Monteral Harrell-Climmons.)

MASON, FOUNDER OF THE CHURCH OF GOD IN CHRIST, 1950S. Bishop Charles Harrison Mason was born on September 8, 1864, to former slaves Jerry and Eliza Mason in Shelby County, Tennessee. He was the founder and first senior bishop of the Church of God in Christ. It developed into what is today the largest Pentecostal denomination and one of the largest predominantly African American Christian denominations in the United States. (Grace Belvin Walker Perry.)

BISHOP WILLIE AND MISSIONARY ALMA RICHARDSON GORDON. Willie Gordon was bishop emeritus of the Louisiana East First Ecclesiastical Jurisdiction for 21 years and served as pastor of Reimer-Gordon Temple Church of God in Christ for 69 years. Missionary Alma Richardson Gordon was known to wear beautiful hats, and her family enjoyed her freshly baked jelly cakes. (Cletis Gordon Sr.)

61

ST. PAUL THIRD DISTRICT BOGUE CHITTO. There are two St. Paul churches in Tangipahoa Parish. One is located in Independence and one in Hammond. (Fairy Dean Cutrer Hannibal.)

ROCKY HILL AME CHURCH, 2000. On December 29, 1874, at the St. Helena Parish Clerk of Court's office in Greensburg, 15 acres were donated to erect a church and a black school. The donation was accepted by William Woolridge, Richmond Terrill, and Madison Prescott. Rev. E.D. Singleton started the church with a small group of members. Carpenter Willie Ginn built the church, which was finished by Rev. Thomas Tucker. (Antoinette Harrell.)

BIG ZION AME CHURCH, 2017. Solomon Johnson's brush arbor was the beginning of the church known today as the Big Zion Church, which in the beginning was known as the Roseland Methodist Church. In 1865, Bishop Clinton set apart the Louisiana Conference of the African Methodist Episcopal Church with three churches: Big Zion, Butler Chapel (started by the Butler family in Amite), and Tasker Chapel AME Zion Church in Ponchatoula. (Antoinette Harrell.)

LITTLE BETHEL BAPTISMAL, 1960s–1970s. Members of Little Bethel Baptist Church often use the Amite River to baptize their members. Outdoor baptisms were once common in the South. (Glyniss Vernon Gordon.)

Bishop Charles Henry Gordon, 2017. The son of Bishop Willie K. Gordon Sr. and missionary Alma Richardson Gordon, Bishop Charles Gordon is the pastor of Richardson Chapel Church of God in Christ in Baton Rouge. He graduated from Westside High School in 1957. He married Wardine Mabry, and they had four daughters, Cheryl, Alma, Debra, and Ursula. In 1975, he earned a bachelor of arts degree in math and science and became an educator in the Tangipahoa Parish school system. (Antoinette Harrell.)

Rev. Wesley Nolan, 1920s–1930s. The Nolan family came from Mississippi, where Wesley was born in 1860. In 1910, his wife died. Two of his daughters, Minnie and Ada, married two Harrell brothers, Edgar and Shelton Harrell. (Antoinette Harrell.)

Four

THEY SERVED, FOUGHT, AND DIED IN THE MILITARY

The military history of African Americans spans from the arrival of the first enslaved Africans to the present day. Men in Tangipahoa and St. Helena Parishes participated in the Revolutionary War, the War of 1812, the Mexican-American War, the Civil War, the Spanish-American War, World Wars I and II, the Korean War, the Vietnam War, the Gulf War, and the wars in Iraq and Afghanistan.

During the wars, African American servicemen faced discrimination within the United States. During World Wars I and II, they did not have equal rights but wanted to serve their country. At home, they were not allowed to enter the front doors of public places and faced segregation everywhere. Some have said they felt like they were fighting two wars.

During the Civil War, 186,097 African American men (7,122 officers, 178,975 enlisted), comprising 163 units, served in the Union army, and many other African Americans served in the Union navy. Several Northern states, including New York and Pennsylvania, recruited entire regiments of African American soldiers, and even some Southern states, like Louisiana and North Carolina, enlisted African American soldiers.

ELDER FRANK HARRELL SR., 1950S.
Frank Harrell served in the Korean War.
He was born around 1937 in Amite
and was a truck driver by occupation in
New Orleans and an ordained minister
of the gospel. (Isabel Harrell.)

PERCY HARRISON, 1942. Percy was
born in 1912 in Tangipahoa Parish. He
enlisted in the US Army as a private
in 1942. He was the adopted son of
Willie and Ella Harrell Harrison.
(Monteral Harrell-Climmons.)

Fred McCoy, 1950s. McCoy served in Japan during the Korean War. After receiving an honorable discharge, he returned home only to fight a different kind of war called racism. He had to fight the Tangipahoa Parish school system during integration. McCoy put his life and the life of his family on the line for justice and equality for the students and African American educators and employees in the school system. (Vernia McCoy.)

Fred Wheeler, 1945. Born in 1911, Fred Wheeler fought in World War II as a sharpshooter. After returning home, he worked on a truck farm in Amite. He was married to Annie Cook. (Earl Wheeler.)

Rev. Raymond Foster Sr. A lifelong native of Amite, Foster served in the US Navy from 1965 to 1969. He is the pastor of Mount Zion Freewill Baptist Church in Montpelier. He was employed at the Tangipahoa Parish assessor office in Amite until he retired. (Rev. Raymond Foster Sr.)

Adam Gordon, 1960s. Adam Gordon served in the US Army during the Vietnam War, and after returning home, protested for better jobs for African Americans. He and his wife, Glyniss Vernon Gordon, opened several businesses. They had two sons, Vernon and Christopher Gordon. (Glyniss Vernon Gordon.)

IRIDIES CAIN, WORLD WAR II. Cain was from Sorento, Louisiana. Some of his offspring made their way to Ponchatoula. (Dr. Kingsley B. Garrison.)

CLARENCE E. HARRELL, 1940s. Born in 1925 in New Orleans to Edgar and Minnie Nolan Harrell, Clarence enlisted and served as a private in the US Army for the duration of World War II. His civilian occupation was a carpenter's apprentice for the New Orleans Housing Authority. He did not have any children, though he was married twice. He had one sister, Juanita Harrell Stewart. (Antoinette Harrell.)

THOMAS PUGH, 1950S–1960S. Thomas Pugh came from a family of musicians and played music for entertainment in the military. He once opened for Elvis Presley. He and several of his siblings learned to play instruments from their father. (Carrie Pugh-Paul.)

DR. FRANK GORDON, 1950S–1960S. In 1956, Frank Gordon earned a bachelor of science degree in vocational agriculture and was commissioned as an officer in US Army. He was stationed at Fort Eustis, Virginia. As a second lieutenant, he served as transportation coordinator responsible for managing a vast fleet of Army vehicles. He also earned a doctorate in theology at the Southern Baptist Theological Seminary in Tallahassee. In 1988, he was elected as the first African American city councilman in Gonzales, Louisiana, and served three consecutive four-year terms. (Shan Gordon.)

WILLARD VERNON, EARLY 1940S, AND PHIL GARRISON, 1914. Rev. Dr. Willard Vernon (left) was born in Roseland to Rev. James R. Vernon and Pearlie Briggs Vernon on August 5, 1918. He attended elementary and high school in Tangipahoa Parish and graduated from Southern University with a bachelor's degree in agriculture education and worked toward a master's degree at Louisiana State University and the University of Southern Louisiana. He was a World War II veteran and taught in the public school system for 24 years. Dr. Vernon died on October 5, 1994. Phil Garrison (right) was born in St. James Parish to Paul and Eave Garrison in 1889. He later migrated to Ponchatoula. He was employed as a machinist at Louisiana Sawmill Company in Ponchatoula. (left, Glyniss Vernon Gordon; right, Dr. Kingsley B. Garrison.)

DR. KINGSLEY BLAINE GARRISON, 1950S. The son of Rev. Phillip Lucien Garrison and Josie "Madie" Cain Garrison of Ponchatoula, Dr. Kingsley Blaine Garrison (far left) lived in the Old Brickyard community. He attended Dillard University for his bachelor of arts degree and Southern University for his master's degree. He graduated from Southeastern University in Hammond with an education specialist degree and received a doctorate in philosophy from the University of Southern Mississippi. He taught in the Tangipahoa school system. He married Della Mae Wooldridge-Garrison; they have one daughter, Leslie Lynette Garrison, and one grandson, Chandler Wilson Garrison. (Dr. Kingsley B. Garrison.)

RAYMOND JOHNNY HARRELL SR., 1960S, AND EDGAR HARRELL, 1919. Raymond (left) was born in Amite. After returning home from Vietnam, he had numerous occupations and became an ordained minister. He is the father of Monteral Harrell-Climmons and Raymond Harrell Jr. Edgar (right) was born in 1896. During World War I, he served as a private in the US Army with the Infantry Headquarters Company, 806th Pioneer Infantry. After he was discharged, he made his home in New Orleans and became a carpenter. He was a Mason. (Both, Monteral Harrell-Climmons.)

WILLIE K. GORDON JR., EARLY 1950S. Gordon was an educator in the Tangipahoa Parish school system. He was known for his delicious barbecue goat sandwiches. He married Priscilla Pope, and they had one daughter, Renee Gordon. (Shan Gordon.)

Five

CIVIL RIGHTS LEADERS AND AFRICAN AMERICAN POLITICIANS

There are many civil rights leaders and activists in Tangipahoa and St. Helena Parishes who have stood up against social injustices and fought for a better quality of life for African American citizens in the two parishes. Some are known, and many are unknown. They boycotted, marched, and organized with civil disobedience tactics in the face of racism and oppression. They changed history and left an impact on many in both parishes today.

Notable civil rights leaders include Annie Lee Hurst, Georgia Gordon Brumfield, Lawrence and Arizona Bryant Spears, Pearl Hunter, Adam and Glyniss Vernon Gordon, Johnny Duncan, Pat Morris, M.C. Moore, Willie K. Temple, Jasper Harrell Sr., Fred and Vernia McCoy, Dr. Kingsley Blaine Garrison, Prince Melson Lee, Wilbert and Earline Dangerfield, and Gideon Carter Sr. These are only a few of the African American civil rights leaders who changed the course of history in the two parishes through their activism. The unsung heroes' and heroines' names may not be in history textbooks, but their contributions to the fight for equality changed the lives of many people for generations to come.

Others were elected and appointed officials who championed the cause of equality as politicians. They worked for social change and justice from the positions they held.

WILBERT DANGERFIELD, 2000s. Dangerfield dedicated most of his adult life to community service. He attended Hammond public school and graduated from Greensville Park High School in 1956. He served two years in the US Army, including 18 months in the Panama Canal Zone. When he returned to the United States in 1959, he married and began his public life. His first political activity was to join the A.Z. Young march from Bogalusa to the state capitol in Baton Rouge in the mid-1960s. Dangerfield helped organize a boycott against A&P to convince management to hire minorities. The picket lasted almost three months. (Earlene Dangerfield.)

MOORE v. TANGIPAHOA PARISH SCHOOL BOARD

• 1954 – The decision is made in Brown v. of education that "separate but equal" violates the 14th Amendment.

• 1956– Fannie Mae Moore of Hammond is placed on academic probation at Southern University and the her father, M.C. Moore, realizes she had not received and adequate secondary school education.

• 1964– President Lyndon B. Johnson signs the Civil Rights Act outlawing racial discrimination.

• May 1965–– M.C. Moore files his desegregation lawsuit is U.S. federal district court in New Orleans.

• July 1965––Intimidation turns violent as bullets are fired at the Moore home in Hammond.

• 1967––Federal Judge Alvin Benjamin Rubin charges the desegregation Parish School Board to integrate local schools and calls for creation of a desegregation plan.

• Mid-1970s––The desegregation Parish School Board agrees to meet a 40-60 ratio of black-to-white system personnel.

• 2006– After years of desegregation order not being enforced, a federal judge hears the local NAACP's protest of the hiring of a white football coach at Ambit High School and orders the rezoning of Moore v. TPSP.

• 2010––Federal Judge Ivan Lemelle calls for implementation of magnet

M.C. MOORE. M.C. Moore filed a desegregation lawsuit against the Tangipahoa Parish school system in 1969. The lawsuit was initially filed on behalf of his daughter, Fannie Moore, who was not given an opportunity to receive the equitable and fair education guaranteed under the 14th Amendment. Moore's home was shot at, and the bullet hole is still visible today. (Moore family.)

HAROLD SMITH AND ANN SMITH, 2000.
Harold J. Smith received his bachelor's
degree in 1971 and his master's degree in
education in 1973, both from Southern
University. He served as a social studies
teacher and coach at Woodland and
Kentwood High Schools. He also worked
as assistant principal at Kentwood High
School and principal at Chesbrough
Elementary School. He served 12 years
on the Kentwood Town Council and
was president of the Tangipahoa Parish
School Board Principals and Supervisors
Association. He was the first African
American elected mayor in the town
of Kentwood, in 2003. (Ann Smith.)

HON. LIONEL WELLS, 2000. Lionel Wells
was the chairman for the Tangipahoa
Parish Council District 7. (Lionel Wells.)

HON. LOUIS "NICK" JOSEPH. Joseph represented Tangipahoa Parish Council District 4. He worked with the other parish councilmen to build a new library in Kentwood. They formed the Tangi-Clean anti-litter campaign and participated in the council's food distribution program during Thanksgiving. Joseph served on the Parish Library Board and on the Veteran's Affairs Committee for the Louisiana Police Jury Association. He retired from the Louisiana Army National Guard and from the Tangipahoa Parish school system as a superintendent in 2007. (Antoinette Harrell.)

MAYOR IRMA THOMPSON GORDON, 2000. Irma Gordon became the first female mayor of Kentwood in 2014. She retired from the Tangipahoa Parish school system after dedicating 30 years to educating children. She served on the Kentwood City Council for 20 years, 16 of which with the position of mayor pro tem. From left to right are Councilman Gary Callahan, Councilman Paul Stewart, Councilwoman Irma Clines, Mayor Gordon, Councilman Michael Hall, and Councilman Terrell Hookfin. (Mayor Irma T. Gordon.)

JOELLE LACOSTE, 50TH ANNIVERSARY OF THE MARCH ON WASHINGTON. Joelle Lacoste is one of the youngest activists in the parish. Her artwork for justice has been featured in many national publications. She attended the 50th anniversary of the March on Washington in 2013. Lacoste has also worked to seek justice for the boys who were abused at the infamous Arthur G. Dozier Reform School in Marianna, Florida. (Antoinette Harrell.)

HON. LEMAR MARSHALL, HAMMOND CITY COUNCILMEMBER. Marshall started the Hammond Youth Education Alliance, became a White-Riley-Peterson Fellow studying afterschool policy at the Riley Institute at Furman University, and started two pilot sites for the launch of Hammond's citywide afterschool program. He is the first African American elected to Hammond City District 4 (in 2010) and the first African American president of the Hammond Chamber of Commerce. (Lemar Marshall.)

JASPER HARRELL SR., 1930s. Jasper Harrell was a strong advocate for registering African Americans to vote and took people to the polls in his pickup truck. His granddaughter Jo-Ann Lewis Frazier tells of the time a man was being lynched in Amite, and the man asked for Jasper. He wanted Jasper to take his shoes and give them to his family. Jasper was often called on to be a mediator. When there was a family crisis, he would take it upon himself to help his extended family. He was a carpenter and a deacon at Gordon Chapel Church of God in Christ. He married Josephine Richardson, and they had 10 children: Catherine, Jasper, Roosevelt, Frank, Isabel, Leon Charles, Henry, Herbert, Raymond, and Deloris. (Monteral Harrell-Climmons.)

LARRY CHARLES FREEMAN, 2017. Freeman is a local small farmer in St. Helena Parish, where he was born and raised. His family purchased a large tract of land in St. Helena in the late 1800s, and the land still belongs to their family today. Larry was elected justice of the peace for St. Helena Parish Ward 5 in 2002. (Antoinette Harrell.)

St. Helena Boycott and Protestors. Annie Lee Hurst (left) and Gloria Gordon Brumfield (right) were part of integrating St. Helena Parish schools and protesting for the right to vote in the parish. (Antoinette Harrell.)

Chief Mike Kazerooni. Michael P. Kazerooni Sr., the police chief for Kentwood, was appointed to the Louisiana Highway Safety Commission as an at-large member in 2016. (Antoinette Harrell.)

CONSTABLE LEMMIE CHAPMAN III. Lemmie Chapman III, a constable for the town of Kentwood, is a strong advocate against litter on the north end of the parish. (Antoinette Harrell.)

COUNCILMAN JONATHAN FOSTER SR. Jonathan Foster (far right) has represented District 2 on the Amite City Council for 24 years. Pictured with him are, from left to right, unidentified, Earl Lee Richardson Sr., and Arthur Hickerson. (Jonathan Foster Sr.)

MAYOR WANDA MCCOY. Wanda McCoy has lived in the town of Roseland all her life, and her family has lived in Roseland for decades. She is the youngest of Ernest and Ardamese McCoy's nine children. She attended school at Big Zion and then went to Roseland Elementary after schools integrated. She continues to work in the property tax department of the sheriff's office collecting taxes while also serving as mayor. She is pictured with Louisiana governor John Bel Edwards. (Wanda McCoy.)

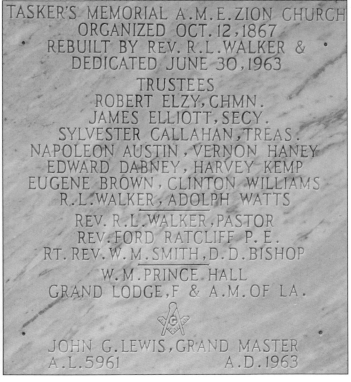

TASKER'S MEMORIAL AME ZION CHURCH. Rev. Arthur Tasker was elected to serve his first of two terms as mayor of Ponchatoula in September 1873. He married a woman named Sarah. He was a very prominent man during Reconstruction who taught the gospel to the freedmen in and around Ponchatoula. On October 12, 1867, he established a church. This was the year that the African Methodist Episcopal Church was established throughout the parish of Tangipahoa. The church was also used as a school. Churches were the first schools for many African Americans in rural towns across the state. (Antoinette Harrell.)

81

OLIVER JACKSON JR., 2000. Oliver Jackson serves on the board of the St. Helena Multipurpose Center. The $900,000 center sits on 40 acres and is under the direction of the parish's 5th Ward Recreation District. Oliver is pictured with his wife, Pat. (Antoinette Harrell.)

WALTER DANIELS. A Democratic representative from Amite for District A on the Tangipahoa Parish School Board, Walter Daniels also served on the Amite City Council and was the mayor pro tem. (Ann Smith.)

LONGTIME ACTIVIST CARL GALMON, 2000. Carl Galmon has family in St. Helena and Tangipahoa Parishes. He is a member of Citizens of Action League. He fought to change the schools in New Orleans that were named after slaveholders. Galmon appears on *Nurturing Our Roots* with host and producer Antoinette Harrell. (Antoinette Harrell.)

HON. MILDRED CYPRIAN, CLERK OF COURT, ST. HELENA, 2000. Mildred Cyprian was elected to the clerk of court for a second term. She is the second African American female to hold that position, having first been elected in 2010. Before she was elected, Beverly Gordon held this office. (Antoinette Harrell.)

ATTORNEY GEORGE TUCKER, 2000. George Tucker had practiced criminal law for over 20 years. He grew up in St. Helena Parish and was the first African American from Greensburg to graduate from law school. He started his career at the Cunningham & Associates in Baton Rouge. Now he has his own law firm at 124 Southwest Railroad Avenue in Hammond. (George Tucker.)

MAYOR TRASHICA ROBINSON, VILLAGE OF TANGIPAHOA. On December 10, 2016, the day of her commencement ceremonies at Southeastern, Trashica Robinson learned that she was elected mayor of her hometown, the village of Tangipahoa. (Trashica A. Robinson.)

LAWERENCE AND ARZIONA SPEARS. This couple has dedicated their lives as civil rights activists. Fighting for basic human rights for citizens of St. Helena Parish, they were instrumental in getting voting rights for African Americans in the parish. They have worked alongside other civil rights activists, including Lola D. Stallsworth, Johnny H. Hall, Ellis Howard, Clarence Knighten, Arizona's mother Pearl Hunter Bryant, her aunt Martha Thompson, and Eunice Paddio. (Arziona "Tat" Spears.)

CIVIL RIGHT ACTIVIST PEARL HUNTER BRYANT, 1960s–1970s. Bryant was a well-known civil rights leader in St. Helena Parish who helped organize voter registration for African Americans. Members of the Congress for Racial Equality stayed in her home as they organized. She went to different cities to protest. Her family was one of the six to integrate in the schools in the parish. When she passed away in 1983, Julian Bond and Andrew Young attended her funeral. (Arziona "Tat" Spears.)

SUPT. JIMMY A. RICHARDSON SR., 2000s. Richardson represented District A on the Tangipahoa Parish School Board from 1994 to 2006. The first plan of action taken by him was launched in 2006 to end the Joyce Marie Moore desegregation lawsuit filed in federal court against the board more than 46 years ago. He is a Church of God in Christ pastor in Kentwood and Roseland. Richardson has been employed in the St. Charles Parish and Tangipahoa Parish school system. (Supt. Jimmy A. Richardson.)

PAT MORRIS, NAACP PRESIDENT OF TANGIPAHOA PARISH, 2016. Pat Morris was the president of the Tangipahoa Parish chapter of the NAACP. She has spent most of her adult life involved in the desegregation battle. From left to right are Osa Bett-Williams, attorney Vanessa Williams, and Pat Morris. (Pat Morris.)

GLYNISS VERNON GORDON, 2015. An educator in the Tangipahoa Parish school system, Glyniss Vernon Gordon was the first African American woman elected to the Amite City Council, in 1982. She was also a businesswoman, activist, and community organizer. (Antoinette Harrell.)

TANGIPAHOA PARISH AMBASSADORS TRAVEL TO WASHINGTON, DC, 2013. From left to right, Katelyn Jones, La'Daesha Lee, Imani Blossom, Aurie Gordon, Jo'Elle LaCoste, and Madison Hill had a first-hand lesson in marching for justice. They proudly carried their signs to stand for change in their communities to the 50th anniversary of the March on Washington. (Antoinette Harrell.)

M.C. Moore Family, Activists, 2000s. M.C. Moore filed a civil suit against the Tangipahoa Parish School Board in 1965 to fight for desegregation and to ensure equality for all children and employees in the school system. On May 3, 2015, the lawsuit turned 50 with no resolution. Pictured are the children of M.C. Moore including Joyce Marie Moore at center holding the proclamation. (Antoinette Harrell.)

Mae Louise Miller, 2000s. Mae Louise Miller (center) was held as a slave in Gillsburg, Mississippi, until 1963. She escaped one night with others in her family. Her story has been featured in *People* magazine, *Nightline News*, and many other media. Pictured with her are Antoinette Harrell (left) and Susan Taylor (right), editor, writer, journalist, and founder and chief executive officer of the National CARES Mentoring Movement. (Walter C. Black Sr.)

Six

WOMEN AND MEN OF
TANGIPAHOA AND
ST. HELENA PARISHES

The two parishes are home to many African American men and women of character. They are the trailblazers who stood the test of time. From the first African American to earn a degree or open a business, to the educators, mentors, leaders, and activists who fought racial discrimination, they became distinguished leaders. They served their communities and parishes to make life better for African American people who were oppressed and faced prejudice. It is important to look back at these brave women and men. This chapter will highlight just a few of the trailblazers.

These unsung men and women had to overcome countless obstacles but were determined to be the examples for what could be accomplished. They set the standards and raised the bar, and they would not settle for anything less.

Black History Month celebrates and reflects on national leaders and their victories. This book is designed to educate readers about their rich local history and the men and women whose names are not written in the history books. Their works and actions have impacted many lives for generations to come. During an interview with a civil rights leader in St. Helena Parish, the author learned that Julian Bond and Andrew Young attended the funeral services of Pearl Bryant.

Another trailblazer, Prince Estella Melson Lee, was honored during the Tribute to Negro Women Fighters for Freedom at the August 28, 1963, March on Washington for Jobs and Freedom. Along with Prince, five other women were honored: Daisy Bates, Diane Nash Bevel, Myrlie Evers (the wife of Medgar Evers), Rosa Parks, and Gloria Richardson.

Jasper Harrell Sr. used his old pickup truck to take African Americans to the voting polls. In St. Helena Parish, seven families fought to integrate schools. Collis Temple Sr. refused to allow his children to attend a fair in Tangipahoa Parish on the day designated as "Nigger Day;" instead, he started a fair at O.W. Dillon School and invited one of America's most significant African American gospel singers, Mahalia Jackson, to perform.

JOSEPHINE RICHARDSON HARRELL AND FAMILY, 1960s. Josephine, born in St. Helena Parish in 1913, was a homemaker and was affectionately called "Phine" by her family and friends. One of her favorite pastimes was working in her flower garden. She enjoyed baking pies and cakes for her family on Sundays. Her youngest child, Deloris, and her sister Rosabel Richardson Moore are pictured. (Monteral Harrell-Climmons.)

ETHEL TEMPLE, 1950s–1960s. Ethel was born in St. Helena Parish. After she married Walter Temple, she moved to New Orleans. She was the mother of three sons: Oliver Jackson Jr., Johnell Temple, and Cleveland Temple. (Ruth Landrew Jackson.)

SHIRLEY CROSS TEMPLE, 1990s. Upon completing 11th grade, Shirley entered the Tuskegee Institute, completed her 12th year of schooling, and subsequently completed her bachelor of arts degree. She was a member of the Tuskegee 100 Choir, serving as secretary for four years. Shirley often talked about her choir director, William L. Dawson, and the fact that one of the choir's most exciting tours was performing for Pres. Franklin D. Roosevelt at the White House. Shirley served George Washington Carver while working at the college dining hall. She also recounted the memorable occasions when she and other Tuskegee students attended programs to hear inspiring lectures from such notable speakers as Mary McLeod Bethune. (Marcia Wilson.)

AMANDA BRELAND RICHARDSON, 1920s–1930s. She was born in 1862 in Livingston Parish, a year before the Emancipation Proclamation abolished slavery. She was married to Thomas Richardson, and they had five children: Annie, Thomas, Golene, Sophia, and John. (Luella Vining Franklin.)

COSMETOLOGIST CLASS, 1960S.
The women who posed for this
photograph graduated from
cosmetology school. Yvonne Collins
is on the left. (Yvonne Collins.)

LETTIE CUTRER ANDERSON, 1990S.
Lettie Cutrer Anderson (left) was a
nurse for the first African American
doctor in Tangipahoa Parish, Walter
A. Reed. The granddaughter of
Robert "Free Bob" Vernon, Anderson
says she worked downtown on
Thomas Street for more than 50
years, including about 25 years for
the doctor and then 27 years for
the South Central Bell Telephone
Company. Today, she can be seen
walking along the street to pay a
bill at Central Drugs or shop at
the other downtown businesses.
(Fairy Dean Cutrer Hannibal.)

ROSE GARDEN CLUB, 1950S–1960S. The Rose Garden Club was started in Kentwood. Among those pictured in the first row are Shirley Temple, Helen Imes, Odeal Thomas, and May Hall. In the second row are Ms. Parker, Ms. Dancer, Ms. Butler, Bernice Smith, Ruby Hookfin, Alta Smith, Ann Gordon, and Meytis Gibson. (Myrtle Cook.)

RUTH TAYLOR JOHNSON, 1980S. Ruth was a midwife in St. Helena Parish. (Earl Wheeler.)

Eva Higginbotham, 1980s. Eva was born in 1904 in St. Helena Parish. She raised over 400 chickens and sold her eggs locally. She is known for the homemade bonnets she wore and her many purses. (Monteral Harrell-Climmons.)

Malinda Lawson, 1920s. Malinda Lawson (center) was the daughter of "Indian Tom" Swain. The author's cousin Andre Richardson is the grandson of one of Esau and Malinda Lawson's daughters and told the author about Malinda Lawson. The descendants of Indian Tom can still be found in the Rieds community. Mark Conley relates that there was a Choctaw Theater in Amite. (Andre Richardson.)

WILLIE MAE AUGUSTINE, 1960s. She worked a secretary before becoming an educator. (Helen Perry Edwards.)

MAMIE HOLMES, 2000. Mamie was known for the delicious homemade tea cakes that she enjoyed baking for her friends and family. Tea cakes are part of the African American heritage in the South. (Antoinette Harrell.)

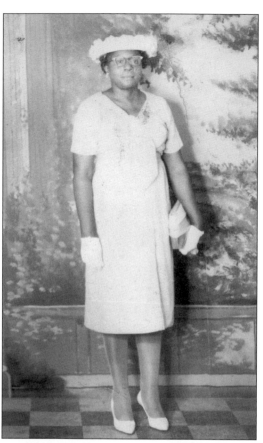

LOIS ATKINS, 1950–1960S. The wife of J.D. Atkins was a woman of influence in St. Helena Parish. (Earl Wheeler.)

WOMEN FOR CHANGE, 2007. This group of women organized a debate for candidates for Louisiana House of Representatives District 72 in Amite. The candidates included future governor John Bel Edwards, attorney George Tucker, and Councilman Walter Daniels. Edwards won the seat. (Antoinette Harrell.)

ALICE IRVING, 1950S–1960S. Alice was one of 11 children born to Susie and Lemuel "Lem" Irving. Her siblings were Lucy, Robert, Thomas, Wilbert, Alma, Ethel, Edward, Lemuel Jr., Ralph, and Roscoe. She also had one stepsister, Luvenia, born to Lem and Millie Harrell. History has it that Lem's given surname was Green but was later changed to his slave name, Irving. Alice met and married Fred Vernon Sr. around 1917 in Roseland. They had five children: Norman, Felton, Fred Jr., Dorothy, and Osborn. Alice and Fred operated a very large farm that required the whole family's participation along with hired help. (Jackie Dukes.)

MIDWIFE MANDY JONES WHEAT, 1950S–1960S. Mandy was born in St. Helena Parish in 1892 to Joe Jones and Lizzie Banks. Mandy delivered thousands of black, white, and Italian babies in Tangipahoa and St. Helena Parishes. People in the community called her "D'Mandie" because she put the letter D before all of her words. She was also known as an herbalist who helped heal many black folks during a time when they could not go to hospitals or clinics because of segregation. Sometimes white physicians would call upon her services to make medicine for their patients. (James Daniels.)

LEONA SPEARS, 1990S. Leona Spears was born in St. Helena Parish. Her husband died in 1943. She was the mother of 12 children and had over 75 grandchildren, great-grandchildren, and great-great-grandchildren. She learned to play several instruments. She was not afraid of hard work and plowed the fields with a mule. She had strong American Indian features. (Lawrence and Arizona Spears.)

MIDWIFE TISHANN WOODS DEEMERS, 1920S–1930S. Tishann was born in 1853 in a small community called Blairtown in East Feliciana, Louisiana. She married Richard Deemer in 1872; their children were Sarah, Richard, Edward, and Ezecial. Her husband was born in 1840 and died on February 25, 1923, in Blairtown. Oral history was passed down to her great-granddaughter Gwendolyn R. Carter. (Gwendolyn Carter.)

ELIZABETH ASHE, 1940S–1950S.
Elizabeth Ashe was a woman of
leadership, poise, and grace. She was
a businesswoman who opened the
first community center and hall for
African Americans in Ponchatoula.
(Ella Mae Ashe Badon.)

**BUSINESS OWNER BELINDA VINING
TREPAGNIER AND FAMILY, 2000S.**
Parishes Supportive Living is located in
Hammond. This organization primarily
provides social services and has been
operating since approximately 2001.
Belinda Trepagnier is at far left in the
first row. (Belinda V. Trepagnier.)

LORRIANE LIZANA, 2000s. Lorriane and her husband, Charles, are the authors of *Authentic Southern Cooking with Chuck and Miss Lorriane: Home Cooking with New Orleans Style Flavor*. They have managed restaurants for 25 years, including Chuck's Soul Food in Pontiac and Chuck's on the Boulevard on South Boulevard in Auburn Hills. (Lorriane Lizana.)

LOUELLA RICHARDSON DEAMER, 1940s–1950s. Louella married Joseph Deamer. They had nine children: Leslie, Ernest, Clara, Ella, Joseph Jr., Leroy, Pearl, Thelma, and Bertha. Joe's nickname was "Bundo." Louella was a homemaker and seamstress. Joe Sr. became an entrepreneur. He was a contractor who provided wooden ties for the railroad. The family moved to the Neola Farm in Amite and later purchased 40 acres in Fluker. Joe raised cotton, sugarcane, and a variety of vegetables. He made syrup and packaged it in tin cans. As a truck farmer, he often drove to New Orleans to sell his products in the French Market. (Lorriane Lizana.)

RUTH LANDREW JACKSON AND HER MOTHER, WILLIE NEAL LANDREW, 1970S–1980S. Ruth was born in McComb, Mississippi. Her family moved to Tangipahoa Parish. She married Oliver Jackson Jr. and had three children. She and her mother are longstanding members of Richardson Deliverance Church of God in Christ in Amite. (Ruth Landrew.)

ZETA PHI BETA. Zeta Phi Beta is an international historically black sorority. In 1920, five women from Howard University envisioned a sorority that would raise the consciousness of their people, encourage the highest standards of scholastic achievement, and foster a greater sense of unity among its members. Pictured are Vernia McCoy (second from left) and Fannie Daniel (third from left). (Vernia McCoy.)

JEANELLE ATKINS RANKIN, 1960s. Jenealle Rankin is the daughter of John David "J.D." Atkins and Louis Johnson Atkins. Her siblings are Deloris Atkins Stuckey, Bernice Atkins Hall, James C. Atkins, and Myrtle Atkins Daniels. Jeanelle was an educator in the St. Helena Parish school system. (Earl Wheeler.)

EVELYN JACKSON. Evelyn was one of 13 children who worked on the 200-plus-acre farm planting, growing, and selling corn, cucumbers, water beans, okra, sugarcane, strawberries, butter beans, potatoes, pecans, sweet potatoes, cotton, and much more. The Jackson family had horses and mules to help plow the fields and raised cattle as well. They would often use their smokehouse to cook meat for sale in addition to homemade syrup, which they also exchanged for work on their farm. (Elisha D. Jackson)

Dr. Garrison and Brothers, 1960s–1970s. The Garrison brothers are pictured attending a funeral service in California. From left to right are Phil Garrison Jr., Dr. Kingsley Blaine Garrison, Binkley Joseph Garrison, and Alphonse Garrison. (Dr. Kingsley B. Garrison.)

Rev. Ernest Thomas Pugh, 1960s. Reverend Pugh was born in 1898 and died in 1979. He received his high school education at Pearl High School in Nashville, Tennessee, and went on to earn a bachelor of science degree from Tennessee State University. He taught school in Tennessee, and through hard work and dedication, was promoted to principal of several elementary and secondary schools in the state. He left Tennessee to take an elementary principal position in Pastoral, Arkansas. He later moved to Amite, where he taught science until his retirement from the Tangipahoa Parish school system. (Carrie Pugh-Paul.)

ALEXANDER HARRELL, 1900s. Alexander Harrell was born in Clinton to Robert and Darska "Dinah" Harrell. He married Emma Mead Harrell, and they had 11 children: Alexander Jr., Alec, Theodore, Warner, Edgar, Henry, Jasper, Palmer, Bertha, Ella, and Virginia. Alexander Sr. and his father purchased 200 acres in Tangipahoa Parish for 50¢ an acre. (Isabel Harrell Cook.)

CHAUNCEY LAWSON, 1930s–1940s. Chauncey was born to Esau and Malinda Lawson in Amite. He opened his own church in a very small, wood-framed building. Inside, one would find a table on which his red phone sat. He used the phone for important calls about astrological signs. Many of the people who attended the church recall him ringing the old church bell. (Andre Richardson.)

DAVID CHARLES REEVES, 1950S. Everyone who worked under this educator's leadership called him Professor Reeves. He was born in Mississippi in 1897 and taught in Ponchatoula. D.C. Reeves Elementary School in Ponchatoula is named in his honor. He was married to Ada Reeves. (Gwendolyn Carter.)

EDDIE PONDS, 2017. The owner of Ponds Enterprises, Eddie Ponds (left) is an educator, photographer, filmmaker, and the publisher of the *Drum* newspaper, the first African American newspaper in Tangipahoa Parish. He is also the host and producer of his own local television program. He taught in the Tangipahoa Parish school system until he retired in 2003. In this picture, he is looking at the *Farmer's Almanac* with local farmer Ernest Frazier. (Antoinette Harrell.)

IVY CUTRER, 1940s–1950s. Ivy Cutrer purchased the first new bus to transport children to Mount Canaan School. According to Grace Belvins Walker Perry, he was very stern. (Grace Belvin Walker Perry.)

WILLIE K. TEMPLE, 1950s. Born in 1933 in Amite, Willie was one of six children born to Charlie Temple and Lena Vining Temple. His siblings were Caretha, Doretha, Maude, Jacob, and Mary. Willie grew up on a 54-acre farm on Bennett Road. His family raised livestock and every kind of produce a farmer could grow. Everyone called him "Pap." Some said they remember him smoking cigars. Isabel Harrell Cook often talked about the role he played in registering African American people to vote. "He drove people to the voting polls," she said. (Edwin Temple.)

LEO COLLINS SR., 1960S–1970S. Leo was born in 1920 in Amite to Abraham Lincoln Collins Sr. and Ima Gene Washington Collins. Leo Collins was united in holy matrimony to Edwina Baker in 1938. His first job was at Gullette Foundry in Amite. He proceeded to do custodial work at Amite High School in the Tangipahoa Parish school system starting in 1945. He also did custodial work for offices. (Yvonne Collins.)

OLIVER WENDELL DILLON, 1950S. Prof. Oliver Wendell Dillon was born on October 15, 1882, and died on May 18, 1954, in Magnolia, Mississippi. He received his bachelor of science degree from Alcorn A&M College in Alcorn, Mississippi, and completed his postgraduate work at Hampton Institute in Hampton, Virginia. The Tangipahoa Parish Training School, founded in 1911, was the first training school for African Americans in the entire South. (Marcia Wilson.)

ARTHUR HARRELL, 2000S. One of Palmer and Manila McCoy's sons, Arthur Harrell was a school bus driver and planted crops. He took the African Ancestry DNA test to find out where in Africa his paternal lineage comes from. His test results connect him to the Mbundu people in Angola. He married Ruth Avant, and they had four children, including Arthur Hickerson. (Antoinette Harrell.)

GIDEON CARTER JR., 1970S–1980S. This educator and community leader was the first African American elected to serve on the Ponchatoula City Council, in the late 1970s. He married Mary, who was also an educator in the Tangipahoa Parish school system. They are the parents of four children: attorney Gideon T. Carter III; Gwendolyn Renee Carter, RN; Genor Carter; and Gemetri Carter. (Gwendolyn Carter.)

RAYMOND WHEELER, 1950s. The son of Joseph and Genora Johnson Wheeler, Raymond graduated from Westside High School. He was a school bus driver and owned his own upholstery shop. (Earl Wheeler.)

ROY CURTIS AND HIS BROTHER J.C. CURTIS, 2000. These two brothers were raised in Fluker. They worked on a farm and sometimes did public work. Roy is pictured at left, and J.C. is at right. (Antoinette Harrell.)

Seven

African American Farmers of the Florida Parishes

The author grew up on land that her maternal great-grandmother purchased in Amite. She was a farmer and worked as hard as any man on a farm, according to her grandson Dan Harrell. One of the author's favorite quotes is by Sojourner Truth: "Ain't I a woman; look at me! Look at my arm! I have ploughed, and planted, and gathered into barns, and no man could head me: And aren't I woman? I could work as much and eat as much as a man—when I can get it!"

Women and men in both parishes worked hard to feed their families and sold what they could to provide for themselves and their families. They worked hard to buy a piece of land to farm. It was not easy for African American farmers: they faced discrimination when trying to sell their produce. Many local farmers relate how they were often cheated and could not get top dollar for their crops like the white farmers did.

Many had to enter the crop lien system, and many farmers lost their land. If they did not own the property, they entered into the sharecropping system. Sharecroppers, tenant farmers, and poor landowners used the crop lien system to borrow money by giving lenders a legal claim to a portion of the crop in advance. When the harvest was poor or prices were low, crop liens led to an endless cycle of debt.

Emma Harrell and her son Jasper entered into this system like so many others. Jasper Harrell worked hard to pay the loans off so that the land could stay in his family. His brother Palmer Harrell lost his land: he purchased a mule he could not pay for, so white men took his property.

W.C. Frazier, Charles Holmes, Eugene Edwards, James Baker, Monroe Perry, Walter Wren Sr., Henry Wheat, Lawrence Spear, and Governor Harrison are just a few of the men who farmed vast acres of land. Mandy Wheat was a farmer and leased her land out to W.C. Frazier to farm. W.C. worked the ground until his health no longer allowed him to farm. Not many young people carry on the trade of farmer any more.

EUGENE EDWARDS, 2000. At the age of 92, Eugene Edwards was still farming—it is in his DNA. When he was a boy, his father hired him out to work on a white man's farm. Eugene prefers to use a mule rather than a tractor. (Antoinette Harrell.)

JAMES BAKER, 2000. Every year in November, James Baker drives from Chicago to St. Helena Parish to make syrup from the sugarcane local farmers grow and harvest. Hundreds of gallons of syrup are made the traditional way. He is considered a master syrup maker. (Antoinette Harrell.)

LAWERENCE SPEARS, 2018. In his 90s, Lawrence Spears is still planting crops. He worked for Kents Enterprises in Kentwood, and also did public work in Baton Rouge. He was an activist and organizer in St. Helena Parish. (Antoinette Harrell.)

ERNEST FRAZIER SR., 2017. Ernest recalls the days when he worked in the field with his father, W.C. Frazier. He started out by watching the smaller children under a tree before he was called to work in the fields with everyone else at the age of about six. He has planted and harvested every kind of produce one would want to eat. He learned everything he knows from his father. (Antoinette Harrell.)

LARRY FREEMAN, 2017. Larry Freeman farmed and raised livestock. He was elected justice of the peace in St. Helena Ward 5. His family is one of the largest African American landowners in St. Helena Parish, and they are still in possession of the land. Larry is seen holding greens he pulled from Craig Coleman's garden. (Antoinette Harrell.)

CHARLES HOLMES, 2000. Charles Holmes can be found planting and harvesting his crops. He shares his produce with the widows and elderly in the community. He often takes a hoe and neatly chops the grass out of his crops. (Antoinette Harrell.)

HENRY WHEAT, 1970S. Henry Wheat was a vegetable farmer. He was a very quiet man and enjoyed working on his farm. He shared vegetables from his garden with the author's family. Sometimes he would let the cows out in the pasture for grazing. Henry was one of many children born to Saul and his wife, Corrine, along with Booker, Rosa, Beatrice, Melisa, Bernice, Myrtle, Bertha, Monroe, Hattie, Mattie, and Roy. (The Wheat family.)

REV. AL SAMPSON, 2009. The president of the National Black Farmers Harvest and Business Trade Cooperative, Reverend Sampson serves on numerous boards and organizations that stress the economic development of the black community. He became involved with the Southern Christian Leadership Conference in 1962 and served as campaign manager for Leroy Johnson, Georgia's first black state senator. Sampson was ordained by Dr. Martin Luther King Jr. at Ebenezer Baptist Church in 1966. (Antoinette Harrell.)

BLACK COWBOYS, 2000. Little is known about the history of black cowboys in Tangipahoa and St. Helena Parishes. Before the trans-Atlantic slave trade, many Africans were herders who owned cattle, camels, goats, sheep, and horses. Herders can be found in every country in Africa. (Walter C. Black Sr.)

J.D. ATKINS, 1980s. Atkins was a farmer and businessman. He owned his own produce packing shed. Often, the African American farmers would get ripped off and cheated. They got a better price when they sold their produce to J.D. Atkins. He rented two spaces at the French Market in New Orleans to sell the produce. (Earl Wheeler.)

LEON DUNN, 2000. Leon Dunn was a truck logger and farmer. In his mid-80s, he still got up on his tractor and planted vegetable seeds. Leon learned everything from his father, Theodore. (Antoinette Harrell.)

WILLARD VERNON, 1960s. Dr. Vernon was man of agriculture and livestock. He loved farming. He is seen here feeding his cows. (Glyniss Vernon Gordon.)

BULL BAKER, 2013. Wanting to learn from the master syrup maker James Baker, Bull would often go out to the sites where James was working. (Antoinette Harrell.)

NEW ORLEANS FRENCH MARKET, 1950s. Rosabel Richardson Moore would go to the French Market in New Orleans to purchase fresh produce. (Monteral Harrell-Climmons.)

Eight

AFRICAN AMERICAN BUSINESSES AND ENTERTAINERS

Robert Zanders played with a band in the local nightclubs. Steptoe's Lounge was no ordinary nightclub, because it was a place where people of color could go and see popular blues artists live. Murphy Steptoe's clientele included teachers, doctors, lawyers, business owners, and common everyday people. It was "high class," and the dress code was semiformal or "church clothes" without the hats. He also sold barbecue, which had a reputation of its own. He prepared the best barbecue ribs and chicken in Louisiana. On Sunday, the club was closed, but he still had a heart to give the people good, quality entertainment. He sponsored baseball games in a field where he had created a diamond.

Another local business was the N.A. James Funeral Home. Joseph Wheeler owned his own trucks. Lem Irving owned a produce packing shed in Roseland, and J.D. Atkins owned another in St. Helena Parish. J.D. Atkins sold produce at the French Market in New Orleans, and also sold to Schwegmann, A&P, and Winn Dixie food stores. Elizabeth Ashe opened a community center in Hammond. Henry Wheat made a living by farming. Other people in the community owned their own beauty shops, sweet shops, and stores. The Womack family in Kentwood owned their own grocery store. A lot of people bartered to survive.

ROBERT ZANDERS, 1950S–1960S. Robert (fourth from left) was born in Amite on December 28, 1910, to Robert and Beatrice Taylor Zanders. He was known throughout the Florida Parishes as a gifted musician and often played for special occasions. In 1974, he was converted during the pastorate of Rev. Francis Williams and brought his music into the church. He served as pianist, president of the senior choir, and member of the Steward Board. He was given the name Gabriel by Bishop Arthur Marshall Jr. due to his inspirational playing on his saxophone. Robert was also a member of the Young Men's Social Club. (Rev. Raymond Foster Sr.)

ROBERT ZANDER BAND. Robert Zanders was the Louis Armstrong of the Florida Parishes. There is not a lot of written information about him, but he is remembered in the oral history of the people who enjoyed him playing his saxophone in the local nightclubs and churches. (Rev. Raymond Foster Sr.)

STEPTOE'S LOUNGE, 1950S. One of the most prominent businessmen in this picture is Murphy Steptoe Sr. Murphy was born in 1906. His mother, Willie, worked as a maid in a private home to support her boys, Murphy, Otis, and her youngest, Sam. Murphy attended school for a while but at 14 began working at a local cotton gin to help support the family. He met Clara Tate in 1924, they dated, and they had a son, M.J. Steptoe, in 1925. (Gloria Steptoe.)

JORDAN PUGH, 1950S. Jordan Pugh and his group get ready to perform. (Carrie Pugh-Paul.)

MOUNT CANAAN MEN'S SINGING GROUP, 1950s. Singing for Christ is something that the men enjoyed doing. Those posing for this picture include some of the Vernon men and Dr. Percy Walker (third from left). (Luther Tolliver.)

PERRY'S DRIVE INN, 1970s. Perry's was owned by Lois and Esther Irving Perry and was an icon in the community. Perry's Drive Inn was the place to be. Glyniss Vernon Gordon recalled that many community and political meetings were held there. (Antoinette Harrell.)

Nine

WHO ARE THEY?

They are the men and women who dared to face the opposition and had the courage to change the face of law enforcement in both parishes. Melvin Finn, Johnell Temple, Oliver Jackson, and other brave women and men were determined to become police and work in the sheriff's office.

Nat Williams was the first African American elected sheriff of St. Helena Parish, in 2007. Michael Martin was chief of operations of the St. Helena Parish Sheriff's Office. Several of the author's relatives are presently employed with Tangipahoa Parish Sheriff's Office and Amite Police Department.

Alex Richardson followed in the footsteps of his father, Pete Richardson, in law enforcement. Reginald Cook is a police officer in the New Orleans Police Department. Alvin Lewis worked in the Passaic County Sheriff's Department in New Jersey as a detective until he retired in 2012.

SHERIFF'S OFFICE, 1960s. Melvin Finn (second from right) was the first African American man hired as a police officer for the Amite Police Department, in the early 1970s. Also pictured are Roger Dangerfield, Alfonse Dillon, and Melvin Finn. (Schirra Finn.)

AMITE POLICE DEPARTMENT, 1960s. These African American women and men worked for the Amite Police Department and the Tangipahoa Parish Sheriff's Office. In the second row at left is Melvin Finn. The lady with the button-down suit is Melva Dillon Brumfield. (Schirra Finn.)

VERA PITTS WHEELER, 2018. Vera graduated from the Tangipahoa Parish school system and is the keeper of the Pitts family history. She comes from a large family. She is married to Earl Wheeler, and they have two daughters. She is a nurse by occupation. (Antoinette Harrell.)

ARTHUR WALLS, MODERN-DAY SLAVE, 2017. Arthur Walls was held on a plantation in Gillsburg, Mississippi, but escaped in 1961. He was featured in a documentary on *Vice* to tell his story publicly. He talks about lynchings and the beatings and abuse he endured as a modern-day slave. (Antoinette Harrell.)

TYREEK FRAZIER. Tyreek Frazier (second from left) received his Eagle Scout badge with four other young men of Troop 263, which meets at DuPage AME Church. Only four percent of Boy Scouts make it to Eagle. These young men are amazing. (Sherry Hudley Frazier.)

HARRELL AND GILMORE, 2018. Antoinette Harrell and Wallace Gilmore got married in Kentwood. From left to right are Ruby Dunn Gilmore, Antoinette Harrell, Wallace Gilmore, Paulette Gilmore Sims, and Thomas Cook. (Antoinette Harrell.)

THE FOUR PILOTS, 2000s. Several young men from Kentwood High School organized a group called the Four Pilots. They help to distribute food, clothing, and other items to the Kentwood community and the Mississippi Delta. The youth are posing for a picture after being guests on NOATV in New Orleans. From left to right are Avery Stickland, Bernard Temple, and Daniel Holmes (far right). (Antoinette Harrell.)

GRANDCHILDREN OF ANTOINETTE HARRELL, 2018. From left to right, Chase, Jo'elle, Carter, and Connor are the grandchildren of Antoinette Harrell. They have traveled to many museums to learn their African American history. (Antoinette Harrell.)

Discover Thousands of Local History Books
Featuring Millions of Vintage Images

Arcadia Publishing, the leading local history publisher in the United States, is committed to making history accessible and meaningful through publishing books that celebrate and preserve the heritage of America's people and places.

Find more books like this at
www.arcadiapublishing.com

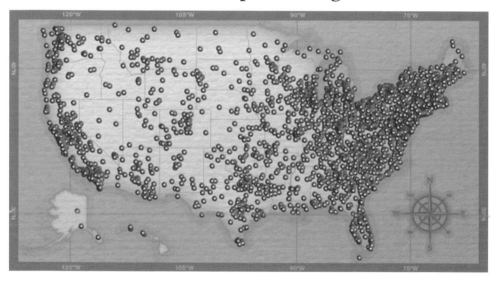

Search for your hometown history, your old
stomping grounds, and even your favorite sports team.

Consistent with our mission to preserve history on a local level, this book was printed in South Carolina on American-made paper and manufactured entirely in the United States. Products carrying the accredited Forest Stewardship Council (FSC) label are printed on 100 percent FSC-certified paper.

MADE IN THE